# MARK HASTINGS

_To Donna._

# THE
# PATHFINDER

**The Pathfinder** by Mark Hastings

ISBN: 9798879415049

Published by:

Mark Hastings

MarkThePoet.Me

For Dad

*"Believe in yourself and all that you are.
Know that there is something inside you
that is greater than any obstacle."*
**– Carl Weathers**


*"Humans can be museums too –
filled with history they can no longer touch."*
**– Bianca Sparacino**


*"Man cannot remake himself without suffering,
for he is both the marble and the sculptor."*
**– Alexis Carrel**


*"Whosoever is delighted in solitude
is either a wild beast or a god."*
**– Aristotle**


*"I don't give up... and it's not out of frustration
and desperation that I don't give up.
I don't give up because I don't give up.
I don't believe in it."*
**– Johnny Cash**


*"Pursue some path, however narrow and crooked,
in which you can walk with love and reverence."*
**– Henry David Thoreau**

# Dear Dad

Whenever a beam of sunlight touches us,
whenever a red-breasted robin
comes to visit us,
whenever we see a white feather
on the path before us,
whenever we feel someone
standing beside us,
whenever we see your face within our mind,
we know that you have returned to us
to make sure we are OK,
as you put your hand upon our shoulders,
as you continue to smile your one of a kind smile,
as your blue eyes continue to shine
brighter than the stars of night sky,
as you continue to give us the gift of you,
as well as your amazing presence and radiating spirit,
as we all continue to feel
your everlasting love.

I cannot believe that it has been
a year since I last saw you,
I cannot believe that it has been
a year since I last heard your voice,
I cannot believe that it has been
a year since I last held your hand;
every day, I still feel our bond and our connection...
every day, I can still feel your presence
and I have felt comforted by the knowledge
that I know you are now living a life
somewhere beyond what can be seen –
because you have visited me
and you have spoken to me
now multiple times in my dreams.

Life will never again
be the same as it was...
every day I think about you,
and I can still recall how
devastated and distraught
I was when I found out
that you had been taken from us...
I am not the same as I was,
nor could anyone hope to be
following the loss of someone
who meant the world to them,
as you will always mean to me...
I will always remember all that
you gave me and all that you taught me,
and I will continue your legacy
for as long as I live...
to me, you will always be
the best father anyone ever had
and you will always be
my inspiration and my hero,
my incredible
and my always near
and dear
Dad.

# The Embodiment of Poetry

I walked into the woods today...
I returned to a place that I know well
and a place that knows me...
I saw the same trees that I have
known for over a decade,
and as soon as I entered the place
where the poet in me was born
I saw echoes of myself from the past –
and I felt as if, once again,
I was seeing a version of myself
who had yet to have suffered
the scars and the losses that I had.

I have always felt blessed with inspiration
whenever I go back to where things began for me –
the place that I have a memory of
which is so clear and special,
the place where I only remember feeling
an abundance of happiness,
the place that I consider
a fountain of poetry,
that I have been back to many times over the years;
however, today, this time,
from the moment that I reentered
the oasis of life that over time
has become the endless kaleidoscope
of memories, experiences,
and thoughts from the moment that I saw it,
I felt as if I were returning
truly changed and different
from who I was when I first visited.

I felt it almost immediately:
I was not the same person as I was,
and yet I was still the same poet
who I have always been –
but now filled with the things
of mine taken from the shadows
of the monuments that define my life...
I felt like I was one of the trees,
and I felt as if they were
as close to me as family...
I felt like I had been waiting for something
which was always there –
but, before today, I could not perceive
what had always been all around me
and right in front of me.

I had been away from this place for a long time –
but as soon as I was once again surrounded
by the storytellers of nature itself,
it did not take me long
to complete the puzzle within me,
by using the pieces I had
left behind from the last time I was there,
to realize that I am,
and I have always been,
what I always wanted to be:
the embodiment of poetry.

# From Time to Time

In white writing
on black leather
I saw the warning
"Nothing lasts forever" –
something I have known all my life,
but recently more acutely than ever.

I have never been blind
to the fact that the universe
is constantly sending us all
messages and signs...
I have never been oblivious
to the fact that some things are created
and some people are
the way that they are
for reasons that might not
become clear for a considerable amount of time.

Sometimes, people do not know
why they chose to make the choices
that they did at a particular moment...
sometimes, people can see
what is to come –
both the good and the bad –
and they decide to proceed anyway,
because we all know that life is
sometimes both scarier than a horror movie
and sometimes ridiculous
enough to make us laugh.

From the day that we are born,
the world changes around us...
from the time that we are grown
and we see, and we understand,
that nothing and no one is meant to be eternal,
we know that there will come
a day when life will go to great
lengths in order to teach us
all a lesson about what matters
when everything is said and done...
we all have to live the life
that was always meant for us.

From what I have seen,
and from what I have learned,
I would say to anyone who
still has no idea what
they are supposed to do
when it comes to making a decision –
whether seemingly insignificant,
or one that is life-changing –
never forget that we are
allowed to make mistakes,
and perhaps repeat the same mistakes over and again.
Why? Because whether we
want to believe it, or not,
each and every one of us is a mystery –
sometimes even to ourselves –
and sometimes the slow discovery
of who we are can make us all feel better
about the most random things in life
that we have accumulated, remembered,
and sometimes we pick out from
our individual internal memory tombola
that we revisit from time to time.

# The Other Side of the World

So many people are looking
for a new beginning...
so many people are in need
of a direction...
so many people wish that they
had something in their lives
that would give them a feeling of belonging...
so many people have friends
and family members who they love –
but they know that what they want
lies beyond what and where
they have always known…
so many people have felt this insatiable
draw to get on a plane and jet off
to somewhere over the horizon…
so many people have this instinct
that compels them to go somewhere
they have never been before,
because the place they are going to
may feel so much like paradise
it could easily be a place within a dream…
so many people are just waiting
for something or someone
to give them the push they need
to take a life-changing leap…
so many people look around at their lives
and they feel that they need more…

so many people do not know
that they have been imprisoned
by something,
someone, somewhere,
for some time,
until they are looking up
at an unbroken blue sky
and they know what it feels like
to be truly free...
so many people have chosen
to do something profoundly special
and adventurous in the pursuit
of finding their life's purpose,
and so many people
have found themselves
choosing to start a new life
thousands of miles away
from the country of their birth
in places that lie far away
on the other side of the world.

# A Matter of Time

I have always revisited the past…
I have always lived in the present…
I have always looked forward to the future –
and there are times when I experience
the past, the present, and the future collide:
as if something momentous has happened,
something revelatory,
something that reminds me,
yet again, that life is, essentially,
multidimensional verses of poetry,
and I get to see and understand things
that I could not and would not
have been able to at any other time –
because I was not ready.

I remember so much…
moments mean more to me than most…
I keep touchstones of experiences
that enable me to travel through time
that can happen as slow and as subtle
as a raindrop falling from above,
or as fast and as forceful as a gust…
I can still recall how people looked,
how places were, what was said,
what song was playing on the radio –
in some cases more than others,
over the timeline of my life –
and when some moments, in particular,
do resurface and come back into focus,
it almost feels as if everything that
has happened and will happen
is all happening all at once.

In some ways, sometimes,
we all must change…
in some ways, sometimes,
we all must break the mould
that we have been cast in…
in some ways, sometimes,
we all must act and not necessarily know
what the next steps to take will be…
in some ways, sometimes,
it is better to not think too much
about what has yet to happen –
and sometimes it is good
to have a goal in front of you to focus on.

We are all pilots, as well as passengers,
traveling through the vortex of time
hoping that one day we will eventually
land and find ourselves somewhere
that will give us what we have been
searching for, without even knowing it…
we are all capable of extraordinary things
and each of us can do something
that uniquely defines us –
and yet, one thing that life teaches all of us
is that the moment that you think
you know it all or have seen it all
you will discover that you don't,
you haven't, you won't, and you can't;
and why?
Because sometimes we are
not meant to know everything –
only what we need to know,
but not always what we want to know;
because everything is a matter of time.

# Everything to Me

On the night after my Dad died,
I ran away into the city –
I wanted to lose myself
within the metropolis of people,
because I felt like I had lost
something inside of me...
on the night after my Dad died,
I walked the illuminated city streets
not knowing where I was going to go,
nor who I was going to meet...
on the night after my Dad died,
I felt more alone than I had ever felt in my life...
on the night after my Dad died,
I wanted to scream, I wanted to shout, I wanted to cry;
but, in all honesty, I could not control my emotion –
so instead I felt numb, but as if I were walking around
with a gaping wound in my chest
that exposed my bleeding heart
that felt like it had been repeatedly
stabbed by a knife.

On the night after my Dad died,
I unexpectedly met some new friends
who all already knew one another
and who had gathered together
to share a Christmas drink –
and though I had never met any of them before
I knew that there was something
to my meeting them that seemed like
someone or something wanted me
to form a brand new link...

on the night after my Dad died,
I remember being angry at whomever
or whatever had taken my Dad away from me...
on the night after my Dad died,
I could not believe what had happened,
nor what I had seen –
and even now, and always,
I will never be able to comprehend
this nightmarish new reality I am living in
that I wish was just a bad dream.

On the night after my Dad died -
after spending most of the night talking,
connecting, and intoxicated, with my new friends –
I said goodbye, and then,
after I somehow made my way home,
I reflected upon what had happened
through a mirrored torrent of tears,
and I wondered what was going to happen next
and who I now was –
and though no clear answers came to me,
I knew that my world, as I knew it,
had come to an end.

My Dad is always with me –
I feel him around me, within me,
like the glow and the feeling
of some kind of perpetual spirit and light
that I know is my Dad speaking to me,
reaching out to me, guiding me,
giving me the gift of his unending love
that will always mean everything to me.

# Shadow of Death

All my footprints have gone...
all my fingerprints have disappeared...
all my impressions have been undone...
all my loves have been lost –
it is as if what happened never happened
and now I am the only one
who remembers or cares
that I once used to be with someone,
sometime, somewhere.

I never used to believe in true endings
until this year,
and now it feel as if life is not done
teaching me the lesson that I, nor anybody,
has true control over what happens...
I never believed that hope would abandon me –
but something is telling me and showing me
that the days of knowing what to do and when
are out of my hands and from now on
I am going to have to do more
to keep the once perpetual light
of optimism within me lit,
because even the most intense
and raging fire can be doused
and can even go out for good.

All my life, I took more
for granted than I realized –
and it is only now, that I am bereft of what
and who I used to rely on,
that I understand where I have been going wrong,
where and when I should have done more,
and made the most of moments
that I thought would last forever,
but were always only temporary...
all my life, I have been blessed
and I have been surrounded
by more than I could have
ever wished or asked for;
and now that things, and people, have left me
I find myself wondering if, when, and how
my life could make sense ever again –
because I have been changed forever
in ways that not even I could describe
or capture in poetry.

The future, to me, is now one day at a time...
the past, to me, is now like somewhere
I once knew that I won't see or repeat again
until I reach my own version of the end...
the present is dark, and even the lights I see,
to me, have lost their once vibrant shine...
reality, for me, has been fractured too badly
for anything or anyone to be able to mend –
because I will always be haunted and living
under the shadow of death.

# No One Is Ever Alone

It's scary how fast time goes by...
It's scary how fast things can change...
It's scary how many times in our lives
we have to say goodbye...
It's scary how many people
have found themselves staring into space,
as they wonder: what's next?

Everybody has a dream that they
hope and pray will become a reality someday...
Everybody has a nightmare that
they wish will never come to pass...
Everybody has an ideal life
that they always imagine,
which within their mind can seem so real
and so tangible that they can almost
make themselves believe
that all they have to do is
simply choose to
get out of their own way...
Everybody has lost someone
who has meant something to them –
and the best way to remember
and to honour someone, in my experience,
is to take the time to stop
what you are doing and realise
that every moment is like a page
being turned in a book,
which soon transitions from being the present
into becoming the past,
which leaves an impression
but not always one that is meant to last.

Life, like the universe,
can seem so big for such a small word...
Life, especially when we are young,
can seem too incredible
and sometimes too unfathomable
for our minds to handle...
Life is a question with an answer –
but you have to stay until the end
in order to find out...
Life is complicated and emotional...
Life is not always good
and life is not always bad...
Life is a riddle that some people
work out slowly but surely,
while others take a more direct approach
and miss the point of why
some things happen
and why some things don't.

A traveller of time and space once said that:
*"Fear can be a superpower"* –
and, if you think back over your life,
and everything that you have been through,
you will realise that though things
might not have gone how you
might once have envisioned they would
things happened the way that they had to,
because life consists of each and every one of us
making a difference and leaping
into the unknown with a secret:
no one is ever alone.

# Never See It Coming

We all cannot help ourselves
from sometimes believing that everything
and everyone will remain
how we have always known them to be...
we all cannot help ourselves
from sometimes taking our eyes
off the road and not always
paying attention to what or who
is approaching us...
we all cannot help ourselves
from sometimes taking things for granted –
like a sacred tree that has stood for centuries
and to its admirers is legendary;
however, then something surprising always happens,
then something shocking will occur,
then something, or someone,
will do something so out of the ordinary
and out of the realms of possibility,
and the world itself can feel to some
as if it has been changed irrevocably.

No one can know with any certainty
what will happen when they leave
their homes every morning...
no one can know what the waves of tomorrow
will take with them, nor what they will bring...
no one can know, by only using their eyes,
who or what is standing right beside them...
no one can know what someone
is thinking and feeling when they look at you,
nor what twists and turns a person will take
driven by the energy of their passion.

There are always plans being drawn up...
there is always intention
that precedes every action...
there are always fragments left over
following an unprecedented
collapse of understanding
which brings to the surface fear,
loss, and uncertainty about the future...
there are always people
coming and going, arriving and leaving –
and though we can all sometimes
make ourselves and others believe
that we are ready for anything,
when something happens
that perhaps feels as impactful
and as disastrous as a star
imploding and then exploding,
when the time comes for us to face
what we may need to face
we will not know what to do,
because when something
of that magnitude happens
we never see it coming.

# The Poetry Only I Could Write

No one is born
with a pen in their hand...
No one is born
with experience in their head...
No one is born
with the knowledge of who they are
and what they are supposed
to do with their life...
No one is born
with all that they could ever need;
however, everybody is born
with the potential to become
anything, or anyone,
and if we are lucky
then we get to be born to,
and brought up with,
parents and guardians who will give us
more than we could ever dream.

I was, I am, and I will always
consider myself one of the lucky ones –
because from the moment of my birth
I was given uncontainable and unconditional love
by my Mum and my Dad...
I was, I am, and I will always be
a dreamer who will do whatever I can
to make whatever I can imagine a reality...
I was, I am, and I will always be
the one who will never allow
darkness to eclipse the light
that throughout everything
I have had to go through
has kept me from going mad...

I was, I am, and I will always be
someone who will never give up
on anything or on anyone
whom to me beams with an ever-glowing
essence of pure joy and poetry.

I have always believed
and I have always shared my belief
that everything happens for a reason...
from the moment that
the wolf within my soul
began howling as a result
of the love that I felt,
which eventually inspired my first poem
and all that have followed,
I knew that I was who
and what I am for a reason...
I have always loved making connections
physically, intellectually, emotionally,
and allowing myself to fall
like a shooting star to Earth
and find myself somewhere
I have always been fated to be
with people whom I have always
been destined to meet...
from the instant that the spark of inspiration
within my mind was ignited,
I have always known that
only I could have seen what I have seen,
only I could have been to where I have been,
and only I can think, imagine, express,
and write the poetry
that only I could write.

# Café Mambo

When I close my eyes, I can still see
the perfectly unbroken blue sky
and I can still feel the peace
and tranquility that I felt within
as I sat looking out at the breathtaking view
of the calming and hypnotic waves of the paradise sea...
I can still recall how lucky I felt
to be where I was, with whom I was with,
as we enjoyed the energy
of the moments of stillness –
as we all experienced the sensation of falling into a trance,
as we listened to the music of the DJ
who seemed to know exactly
what songs to play and when to play them
and who you could tell from the smile on their face
knew that they had the best job, in the best place,
and with one of the best views on Earth
there could ever be...
I can still see the sunlight
sparkling off the spinning mirrored balls...
I can still feel the tender touch of the ocean breeze...
I can still remember what I was thinking
and who I wished were with me,
where I was, so that they, too,
could share what I was feeling with me
that felt more dreamlike
and heavenly than pictures could ever show –
that was what I saw, that was what I felt,
that was what I can still see
and relive within my mind when I close my eyes
and I think about my time
on the island of Ibiza,
at the world famous *Café Mambo*.

# The Insight

My father, my mother,
my family, my friends, and I
have shared many amazing
and wonderful gifts of shared experience together –
however, on more than one occasion,
above all the gifts of reciprocation,
the psychic and empathic bond
that I have had with certain people
still continues to thrill me
and to further convince me
that what we think, what we feel,
what we say, what we share
is sometimes inaudible
and only known by those who
we have opened up to
and those who we have
given a part of our soul.

Since I was a child,
I have put my trust in people...
since I was a child,
I have put my faith in fate...
since I was a child,
I have put my heart into a circle
of family who became my world...
since I was a child,
things have changed in some ways –
whereas, in some ways,
some things have remained the same:
one of which being,
I have always preferred
to be early for something
than to turn up to something, somewhere, late.

I have always had heightened senses
that told me that something was happening
or that something was about to happen,
that though it would be out of my hands
whatever it was would have a profound effect on me...
I have always had this gift
to be able to feel what and who
lies beyond the invisible veil
that separates the different versions
of what is called "reality"...
I have always had this instinct about certain things,
even before I knew what they meant,
and I have had experiences
with certain people when we
gave something to each other,
and I know that what we had –
though perhaps short-lived –
meant something at the time.

I have always loved having the secret knowledge
that I could do the seemingly impossible –
that I could go back to the beginning,
relive moments when I was younger,
and revisit with the people
who mean the most to me,
as well as return to the places
and to revisit the people
I knew from days and relationships gone by,
where, when, and with whom
I am certain I was fated to have known
and to have been given the blessing
of perspective because of
that has only given more power
to my one of a kind insight.

# The Last Sunset

It's OK if I should pass on
to the world to come,
because I can honestly say,
with my hand on my heart,
that I have played my part
and I have definitely left my mark...
it's OK if I had to go
because I would again get to see
all the people whom I have known –
including the man who was always
and who will forever be my hero...
it would be OK I were to have written
my last poem and to have seen my last sunrise,
because I know that I did my best
every day while I was alive...
it would be sad to have to go
and to not be able to say a proper goodbye
to all those people who I know
would miss me when I am gone
and who I know would think of me and cry...
it is not something I am planning to do,
it is not something I am looking forward to,
but if this poem were the last thing
that anybody heard of me
then I hope I will be remembered
as being someone who gave back
and who believed that every day was a gift...

it is my lasting hope and my wish
that someday someone
will read my words,
someone will see my face,
someone will think about something
or about someone who they love
and wonder what and whom
it was who inspired me,
and the future reader of my poetry and I
will begin to communicate with one another
across space and across time
because we will have created
a bridge back to each other
that we can use to learn more
about ourselves and about how we can
all help others through the darkness
that follows the last light
of our last sunset.

# The Dance of Nature

Seeing the fallen conkers
below the tall horse-chestnut trees,
watching the helicopter flight
of the spinning sycamore seeds,
I am always reminded of
the transition of seasons taking place,
and just how breathtaking and beautiful
nature is, always has been,
and always will be to me.

There is always something
in the air at this time of the year –
something ethereal, something magical,
something supernatural...
there is always something
in the way that people
feel drawn to being outside
and exposed to the elements
that points to an underlying
physical and emotional connection
that we all feel and we all want to share
with those who we are closest to.

Since I was a child,
I have always loved the autumnal colours,
the intoxicating smell of the natural world
that lingers after a rainstorm,
the sight of the constellations
of the stars of the night-sky
that somehow shine clearer and brighter
than at any other time,
I have always felt the invigoration
of every one of my senses
influence my thoughts and my dreams –
and the imprint that every transition
that I have witnessed has had on me
has been one that I never expected
and I have never forgotten,
because, as my Dad was aware
and as my Dad always reminded me,
everything and everyone is connected
and we must all do all that we can
to maintain the rhythm and the balance
necessary while participating
in the never-ending dance of nature.

# Ultimate Fate

Sometimes, the more you
think about something,
and sometimes the longer
that you spend obsessing about someone,
in retrospect, you can eventually
come to discover that you could have
spent the time that you did
pursuing what makes you happy –
rather than being held back
by those who never truly will be...
sometimes love can be like a house of cards –
and it can take the removal
of one card out of many
to bring everything crashing down...
sometimes, we can find that we are
putting more effort into a relationship
that our significant partner –
and that is when we can come
to start hearing the alarm bells ring
and start seeing the signs
that point to an instability
within the balance of the necessary
give and take that is essential
and should always be mutual...
sometimes, we can all easily be deceived
into believing a good lie –
because we put all our trust
in someone who from the moment
that we met them made our heart
pulse like the lightning of a thunder cloud...

there is a reason why some things
come easy to some people,
and there is a reason why some things
come harder for others –
but just because something
is effortless, or difficult,
that does not mean that further
effort is not necessary in maintaining
the energy and the momentum of something,
until a transformation occurs
that makes us all naturally reevaluate it...
some things will always change,
some people will always remain the same –
but no matter how
the roll of the dice shakes out,
as long as you can say with
your hand on your heart
that you did your best
and you did all you could,
then nothing and no one
can judge you on something's
ultimate fate.

# Viva Ibiza!

Every morning, as I greeted the new day,
as I looked to the horizon,
as I saw the light of the sunrise
flow over the mountains and the roofs of the houses,
as always, I was in awe...
every morning, as I walked the coastline,
as I listened to the sound of the waves
of the ocean going in and out,
I saw, I heard, I felt the energy
of the cosmic poetry around me
touch me, inspire me, and rejuvenate me...
every morning,
as some of the revelers of the night before
still remained sitting upon the sandy beach,
as the echoes of the beats
of the entrancing music continued to linger,
I witnessed life, people,
attempting to revive and reset themselves
so that Summer's cycle could repeat,
just as it is always expected to...
every evening, as I returned from enjoying
and embracing the experience of being where I was,
on an island of both beauty and infamy,
I always looked forward to looking out,
just as the light of the sun touched the waves of the sea,
as the perpetual celebration of life carried on,
and as I closed my eyes I said to myself
what some may only express silently with a smile
when they find themselves
in a paradise-like place where anyone can do
what they want to do and where anyone can be
who they want to be:
*"Viva Ibiza!"*

39

# Love/Life

Love is a roller-coaster ride of ups and downs...
Love is an adventure of heights and depths...
Love is a storm of emotions...
Love is a sacrifice, a leap,
a promise, a bond, a mutual connection
and a commitment to journey
somewhere with someone, or with something,
that cannot be understood, nor undertaken, alone.

Love is a beginning;
Love can be an end...
Love can be the making;
Love can be the breaking...
Love is what happens
when you choose to take a step
into the unknown with someone
who you feel something for
beyond the limits of just being friends...
Love is about giving, receiving,
caring, listening, learning,
appreciating and not taking for granted what you see,
hear, and feel changing, evolving,
and perennially blossoming.

Love can be tested...
Love can be lost...
Love can be mended...
Love can be harder to define
and to put into words than anything,
because Love is something that seems so simple
from the outside looking in
but which, in reality, is more complex
than the answer to the meaning of life.

# Universal Translation

We all go through life
looking for connections...
we all venture far and wide
searching for similarities...
we all journey to places
hoping to make some happy memories
and to have some fun...
we all trek, voyage,
and ultimately discover,
the deeper that we dive
into the relationships
that define the human adventure,
that the frontier of understanding
is one that is infinite.

I always find it amazing and fascinating
when I meet someone who speaks
one of the same languages that I do –
especially when there is also
a meeting of minds that
instantly and naturally occurs...
I always feel fulfilled
after talking with someone
who I might have just met
who immediately recognizes that
we have something in common
by the recognition of something that I am wearing –
because the near effortlessness
of our communication reminds me
that we are all meant to find people
who we can give back to and can give us
the best of each other's worlds.

I have always been hopeful
and optimistic about the future,
the world, the universe,
the possibilities of everything and everyone...
I have always formed bonds with
fellow enthusiasts of the same things,
the same places, the same areas of interest,
the same sources of escapism and enjoyment...
I have always known
that the only way to find commonalities is to use
the means at your disposal
to look beyond what is going on around you
and follow the steps
to where people like me
wait to be found and reminded
that they are not alone...
I have always believed that
what and whom we choose to engage with
influences us in ways that cannot be quantified –
but the more that we meet and talk
with others who just want to
make the most of what fills them with passion,
we find that we share a dialogue
that will forever be a gift
of universal translation.

# The Dream Team

Sometimes, most of the time,
to complete a task of great importance,
you can only count on the best
of the best to be able to achieve
what must be achieved,
and to do what must be done...
sometimes, most of the time,
you need to call in an "A-Team" of experts and professionals
to push forwards, go beyond the limits,
and not stop until the battle being faced has been won...
sometimes, most of the time,
there is only a small group of colleagues
who have worked together for a long time
who can work together to do the impossible
and turn a bad situation into something good...
sometimes, most of the time,
a certain combination of souls
are the only ones that can rise to the occasion
and ride the waves of a flood...
sometimes, most of the time,
only those who have been sent far and wide,
know what it is like to have to brave
a storm of chaos and leave
as they arrived with their heads held high
with stories of what they have done,
who they have met, and where they have been...
sometimes, most of the time,
when there is trouble happening somewhere
that you know no one else can handle,
why settle for anything less than The Best
when you know that you can always call on,
and you know that you can always count on,
the unparalleled skills of "The Dream Team".

# The Summer Rain

Listening to the summer rain
fall upon the windowpane,
I remember Summer's gone by
when I smiled, and those when I cried...
I remember the sunshine and the love...
I remember the moonlight and the loss...
I remember every moment of connection…
I remember every time I felt as if
everything and everyone was forever –
and I still haven't learned my lesson...
I remember the ups and the downs…
I remember the highs and the lows…
I remember the deep conversations
that I had with people about life,
meaning, poetry, music, and sound –
and I remember time going by
so incomparably and wonderfully slow...
I remember, and I never forget –
that is my curse, and that is because,
at all times, I always try to do my best
to make something last for as long as it possibly can.
The almost hypnotic sound
of countless water-droplets…
the intoxicating smell of a downpour…
the entrancing falling
of the veil of the world itself
opens something within me
to a series of places and faces
that were once my idea of perfection,
but which are now only echoes of the past
that return and then are gone again
like the waterfall of time
of the summer rain.

# The Olympia

From the moment
that I saw it in the window
of the Cancer Research UK charity shop,
I knew that I had to step inside and buy
something that writers have used
for years to type, to print,
and to share their ideas with others
the world over since its invention...
from the moment that I saw
the Olympia typewriter,
I felt as if I were immediately drawn to it
for some reason that I cannot yet explain...
there was something about the Olympia –
something that spoke to me,
as if the typewriter itself
was talking to me, beckoning to me,
to become its new owner
and take it home with me
so that it could be a talisman for me
in all my future literary endeavors...
from the moment that
I stroked my fingers upon
the black keys of the Olympia,
I felt a moment of connection
with whomever it was
the typewriter had previously belonged,
and I knew that I was always
meant to possess it, to use it,
and to take it with me
on the next chapter
of my writing journey.

From the moment that I held
my silver pen that I used
to write hundreds of my poems,
when I first became a writer,
I also remember feeling a similar
impression of instant inspiration –
and that is why I believe that
something wonderful
and transformative awaits me,
and will elevate me
to new heights of poetry,
because I now have
at my fingertips
the totem of my kin
that is my typewriter:
The Olympia.

# Threads

I have always been
a natural detective at heart...
I have always been
appreciative of details –
like the hidden messages
that artists like to weave
within the tapestry of their particular art...
I have always been
an observer of the cosmos...
I have always been of the opinion
that because the universe is so big,
so varied, so full of things
that have happened, and will happen,
that we will never know,
there is no question that
there is no greater mystery
than that of the endless frontier of space.

Not everything is meant to be known;
however, some people will
always want to know as much
as they can about something
that peaks their curiosity...

not everyone can be known
for who and what they are,
nor for what they represent;
however, everybody can become
naturally synonymous with
certain things and with being a certain way
that, over time, people can become
accidentally famous, or even infamous,
simply by being themselves
and doing what they love to do
so effortlessly.

To some people, everything
is about all appearances...
to some people, actions
echo louder than words...
to some people, when they
make their mark upon the world,
it can be hard for them to differentiate
between what they think of themselves
and what opinion other people have of them...
to some people, when they find out
that the world, the universe,
the reality outside their mind
is different than they thought it was
they find themselves reformulating
their idea of what they know
about themselves, as well as about others,
as they follow the clues left behind
of the remaining,
ever-present,
threads.

# The Whole Truth

I have looked into someone's eyes
and I have told them that I loved them –
and, every time I have,
it has felt like an infinite moment of time...
I have listened to someone speak
and I have been so entranced by their voice,
in what I can only describe
as a perfect moment,
that they have made me feel
happier than when I was a child...
I have had experiences
that felt like dreams,
because when I was living
certain moments with certain people
I felt as if I could happily repeat
those same moments over and over again –
because in those moments
I felt comfortable exposing a part of myself
that I do not normally put on show;
however, like most people,
I always leave clues...
I have wondered,
as I have wandered,
why do things happen
when, where, and why they do?
However, I have come to realize
that life has its own plan and story to tell
that only makes sense
if and when you are lucky enough
to get to know the whole truth.

# Meant to Be

I have no children, I have no lineage;
however, what I will one day leave behind
is my books, my poetry –
just like Simon & Garfunkel
once sang about in their song "*I Am A Rock*" –
and that makes me eternally grateful
and profoundly happy.

I have no regrets, I have no wish
to underdo what I have done –
because at the point when I made
the decisions that I have made
I did not think about the end
that would ultimately come to pass
because it had to, because it was always meant to.

I have vivid memories of both
first times and last times
that I saw certain people –
and though the start of something
is always more wonderful
than when it concludes,
I am glad that I have met who
I have met, and I am glad that I have
done what I have done,
I am glad that I have been
to where I have been,
because I am the embodiment of my poetry
and my poetry is the embodiment of me.

I have been embraced;
I have been pushed away;
I have been displaced;
I have been on a lone path
for what feels like forever and a day –
but do you know what?
If given the chance to change something
I would not change a thing,
because everything happens for a reason,
there is no such thing as coincidence,
and because the destiny of all of us
unveils itself and is unique to each of us,
and there is no question in my mind
that you were meant to find me
just as I was meant to meet you.

# Road Trip

Life is complicated...
sometimes there is no way to know
what way is the right way
and what is the wrong way to proceed...
sometimes truly life-changing decisions
are made in the moment
based on timing and instinct –
that is why, sometimes,
getting away from almost everything
and almost everyone,
somewhere different,
is exactly what we all need.

Even machines sometimes
need a "time out" to reset...
even animals sometimes
need to go for a walk
not knowing where they are going,
nor what they are going to find...
even people who like to
"Live in the Fast Lane" would confess
that sometimes even they
have to get some rest...
even people who love being
surrounded by technology
and fully-integrated into
what is going on in culture and society
like it when they can turn everything off
and make the most of the most
precious thing in the universe: time.

Every journey is influenced
by what you do, where you go,
and, most importantly,
who you choose to travel with...
some people we only walk in parallel with
for a short time before our
paths diverge once again
and there is an unmistakable
and inevitable drift...
whether it is at annual family
gatherings and reunions,
or a last-minute thought to do something
you have never done before,
we all are better for any
and every experience that we can share
with those who we cannot wait
to be around and who we miss
more than anything when they have to leave.

Sometimes you can't beat packing a bag,
getting into a vehicle with someone
who might know well –
but who you might not get the opportunity
to spend as much time with as you would like –
and tuning the radio to a station
that always plays songs
that always seem to be able
to read your mind
and tap into the rhythm of your heart,
and talk about the most random of things
like only those who enjoy
spending time with one another can,
and head off towards the sunrise,
or into the sunset,
on an unforgettable
road trip.

# Within Me/Without You

This is the first Father's Day
that my Dad has not been with me
and when I have not been with my Dad...
this is the first Father's Day
that I will be unable to hold my Dad's hand
and give him a well-deserved hug...
this is the first Father's Day
that I won't get to look into
my Dad's blue eyes and see
shining from them a light
of enduring love...
this is the first Father's Day
that I will be unable to see my Dad's smile
and celebrate how amazing a father
he has always been –
and that makes me extremely sad.

Every day, more than anything,
I wish that my Dad was still with us...
this Father's Day, I feel gratitude,
as well as pain –
because I know how lucky I was
that my Dad was my Dad,
but he has passed on
to the world beyond
and because he is no longer
where he always was –
by my side –
there are times when I
look around at the world
and I feel deeply lost.

My father will always be
a force of nature to me –
someone who all my life
has influenced my thoughts and actions,
and who will never stop inspiring me...
my Dad continues to speak to me
through my dreams,
through his teachings,
through what he gifted me,
through the numerous talismans
that he left behind that will
forever tie him to me...
this Father's Day,
I feel as if I am walking in the dark –
but with an ever-glowing light
that all my life has tied me to what
has always been constant and true...
this Father's Day, as well as every day,
I feel, more than words could ever say,
that I can hear the voice of my Dad
within me, guiding me –
and to my Dad, on Father's Day,
I want to say that I love you,
I miss you, and that life will never again
be the same without you.

# The Flash

Whether it is my thoughts, my emotions,
my feelings, or any part of my body –
from my head to my toes –
my mind is, and has always been,
active and racing away with itself...
since I was a child, I have always
been fast on my feet, fast with my fingers,
fast with my legs, fast with my arms –
as if I had an internal lightning-bolt
propelling me that never needed to be recharged...
growing up, the natural spark within me
energized me with this insatiable need for speed
and to break through every one
of the barriers that tried to stop me in my tracks...
I have always had access to this
invisible and yet tangible force
capable of inspiring ideas
as well as giving me all that I needed
to exceed my limits and to reach for the stars...
everybody who has ever known me
would tell you that no matter
what I am putting my heart,
my mind, my body, and my soul into
then I will not slow down, nor deviate,
until I have achieved something
that is beyond what I had intended...
I have learned the hard way that sometimes you have
to make the most of every moment,
as if every experience was your last –
and that is why, just like people, or like instances of time,
now you see me, now you don't,
I am here, there, everywhere,
and then I am gone again in a flash!

# The Dark Side of The Muse

The muse of an artist can be beautiful...
the muse of an artist
can literally radiate with light...
the muse of an artist can
take them to the infinite possibilities
that lie far above the clouds
and beyond the blue...
the muse of an artist
can stay with you your entire life;
however, as with everything
that exists in a state of balance,
where there is light, there is always dark.

Inspiration is everywhere –
in everything, in everyone –
and it can compel artists, especially,
to do many things
and to go to many places
that might, ordinarily,
seem out of character...
inspiration, mixed with intense emotion,
can send those capable of
interpreting the poetry of the world –
in colours, in music, in pictures, or with words –
off on a tangent from which
the road to return might not be
one that is straight and narrow.

Day and night,
the love felt by artists
radiates and echoes
beyond their thoughts and dreams –
and sometimes when an artist
meets someone new,
who immediately touches them
and transfers something
incredible and powerful to them,
a change can be felt, sensed,
read, heard, seen, in everything
that the artist does, and creates;
and when an artist's heart is inevitably broken,
it can feel as if a black hole
has opened up within them,
and they can find themselves
walking a path upon which
they feel as if they no longer
have anything left to lose...
just like the shadow of the moon,
just like someone in a bad mood,
just like the explosive that
ultimately lies at the end of burning fuse –
there is always a light side
and a dark side of the muse.

# Give Poetry A Chance

Some things seem
inaccessible to some people
from the outside looking in...
some people have preconceptions
about some things...
something can sound harder to grasp
than it actually is...
people do not know what they are missing
until they give something a try
and they find themselves
being changed by the experience.

Some people say that
they are simple and predictable –
however, in reality, everybody
is capable of surprising others...
some things that happen in life
feel like something out of a dream,
because they do not make sense...
some people can look at
a priceless piece of art
and feel daunted by its simplicity,
as well as by its obvious complexity,
that they find themselves
feeling feelings they have never felt before...
some people sometimes cannot put into words
what a poem, a painting, a sculpture,
a photograph, a film, a book
is doing to them subconsciously –
but they know that no matter
what they do, and where they go next,
their perception of the world
will forever be changed.

Some things we find
at the same time that they find us...
some people sometimes
want what others have –
but there is always a reason why
some things come easy
to some people, and not to others,
that is out of our hands...
some things never stop being
a rejuvenating resource...
some people do not always know
what they want, nor what they need,
until someone gives them a gift –
and sometimes within
the magic words of a poet
readers can be given a blessing
that is so special it is meant to last;
so, if you ever need energy,
insight, wisdom, beauty,
then you need only
to seek out a poet
give poetry a chance.

# Return of the Poet

Even though, at times, I may have
ventured "Too Close To The Sun",
I will always be the "Poet of the Sphere"...
even though I have written about
"The Wolf in Me", "The Wolf in You",
"The Wolf in Us" and "Vega - The Vampire King",
I will always emanate "The Sound of Mark"...
even though I have been "Playing God",
I will always be "The Eternal Boy"...
I will always be "The Dreamer and The Dream"...
I will always love "Truly Madly Deeply"...
I will always be "The Rambler"...
I will always be the "Poet of the Multiverse"...
I will always be "The Comeback Kid";
because, even though I have stories within me
that I believe are just waiting to be told,
poetry is my life's blood...
poetry is my voice...
poetry is my epic flood.

Poetry is my universe
within which I do not have a choice –
because poetry is my destiny,
it always has been and it always will be...
poetry has brought me gifts of connection...
poetry has always been within me...
there isn't a day that goes by
when I do not open my eyes
and see the light of inspiration...

there isn't a day that goes by
when I do not listen and hear
the rhythm of life's music
in unison with my
multi-layered imagination...
even when things seemed to be
coming to the end of their calling,
I always believed that
whenever the time arose
when I might need
to be renewed,
the one within would climb,
like a "Rising Star",
and there would no longer be any limits –
because, like a shooting star in the night sky,
there would be no stopping
the return of the poet.

# Resource Allocation

Within every living, breathing,
and continuous system on Earth
there is always an allocation of resources...
every day is filled with so much
and with so many people wanting
a piece of the metaphorical pie of life...
everybody wakes up with an agenda –
even those people who say
that they have no plans
are looking and waiting for something
to direct their choices...
everybody has a morning routine;
everybody has an afternoon delight
that they like to indulge in
every now and again;
everybody has an evening of escapism
when, which, and where they can be themselves
without having to wear a disguise.

Even in an orchestra of many players,
of many instruments,
there are those who simply love
the opportunity to play and to perform –
and there are always those
who hope to sit alongside the conductor
and get to do a solo...
there are people who are team players –
but who also like it when they can
be me made to feel special,
when they can make their mark,
and when they can play the tune
that others afterwards
will continue to follow.

63

Nothing is unlimited –
even the time and the light of a star
runs its course and then fades slowly,
until the instance when
its speed and its luminosity
becomes a shadow of its
optimal energy and motion...
there is always a turnaround
of everything – a reconstitution:
when something is taken apart
and then put back together again...
everyone, over the course of every day,
starts in one state of mind
and then transitions into another –
and there is no knowing
what will happen to anybody
during the time that they are
in conscious and physical
contact with the world around them –
because, every day, the world delivers
instances of insight and adaptation
throughout its process of
resource allocation.

# Don't Stop

Don't stop being who you are...
Don't stop being what you are...
Don't stop seeing the world
how you want to see it...
Don't stop reading into
the poetry of everything...
Don't stop giving your all
to who and what matters the most...
Don't worry about tomorrow,
because the now should be your focus...
Don't stop until you reach "The End" –
and, even then, do not believe
that that, as they say, is that –
because, take it from me,
the spirit of something
and someone can never truly be lost.

If you want to do something
for yourself, for those who know you,
for those who can always see
the value of what you do every day,
then be who you want to be –
and, most importantly,
don't stop.

# Out of Your Shell

It is good to challenge ourselves...
it is good to take on new responsibilities...
it is good to do things
we have never done before –
in fact, it is essential in maintaining
our mental health...
it is good to expand our knowledge,
see the sights and meet new people
from different localities...
it is good to be immersed
in the unfamiliar...
it is good to test our tolerances...
it is good to let down our guard
and converse with people
who have different answers
to the question: why are we here?
It is good not to worry
about if someone is watching
and just do your thing –
even if it leads to you involuntarily
making a joke, singing, or starting to dance...
it is good to look the way you want to look...
it is good to have your own opinion
of what is beautiful...
it is good to have an imagination
and to have the gift to be able
to see the faces and to hear the voices
of characters that you read in a book...
it is good to step out of your comfort zone
and embrace the opportunity
to be able to fly free of your nest
and naturally find yourself
coming out of your shell.

# Life's Light

Energy can neither be created nor destroyed,
but energy can change form...
the creation of all things began
billions of years ago,
but nothing is as it was...
people can be emotionally open
and then transition into becoming closed off –
even once open doors can change into becoming walls...
you can prepare for the rest of your life,
but what no one can ever be ready for
is the end of days that follows
a particularly painful absence and loss.

Endings are necessary.
Full stops are essential.
Severance hurts,
but sometimes it can also
be seen as an opportunity.
Everything big
over time transitions back
into becoming small.

Generations leave legacies...
life needs regeneration...
love is a dream...
in order to march every army of ideas
needs the beat of a resounding drum...
time is precious beyond belief...
every day needs a night...
the world is not all that we see...
every exposure is a convergence
and a prism of the fundamental
colours of what makes life's light.

# Walk The Walk

Some people say that they are going to do something,
but they never do...
some people say that they are going to be somewhere,
but they never are...
some people make promises to make something happen,
but they never make the right moves...
some people say that they
are going to make a difference
but they never make their mark.

Talking about something is good...
dreaming about something is wonderful...
one drop of anything can
eventually lead to an epic flood...
believing that someone will be there
for you when you need them is great,
because it is necessary in life
to trust and to have faith in people.

Not everything can happen how we want it to...
sometimes some people are, unfortunately, "all talk"...
not everybody is as forthcoming
about their intentions and motivations,
and sometimes someone who we thought would never change
can surprise us by doing something
we never thought they would do...
in my experience, if and when you can,
you should always endeavor to
be a person of your word,
and when you need to, if you are able,
if you are going to talk the talk
make sure that you also
walk the walk.

# Follow Your Heart

Follow your heart –
even if your head tells you not to.
Follow your heart –
even if you do not at first know
what it wants you to do.
Follow your heart –
because your heart is literally
what drives you.
Follow your heart –
because your heart is
the one thing about you
that has been there for you
and has kept you alive
throughout everything that you
have had to go through.

Our imagination is where we dream
and where we find our ideas
for what we want to make real...
our memories are the roots of the garden
where the flowers of the seasons
to come of our life will grow...
our relationships, how we are perceived,
and how we perceive others,
are what we use to build the picture
within our mind that we hold on to
and constantly refer back to...

our achievements –
personal, as well as professional –
are what act as lighting rods
that ground us whenever we may
find ourselves surrounded by
chaos on an unimaginable scale...
our intentions are not always
going to be selfless,
because everybody is human
and sometimes selfish –
but as long as no harm follows
in the wake of our actions
then we should all sometimes
explore opportunities with the same
enthusiasm of life as that of a child
that can sometimes manifest itself
spontaneously and out of the blue.

There is always a reason for everything...
There has to be more than meets the eye...
There is always something that
captures our imagination
more so than something else...
There has to be a first,
and there has to be a last –
but in between those two extremes
there will always exist a world
of possibilities and poetry
where and when so much can be
witnessed, felt, read, heard,
thought about, and dreamt of...
there is so much that you can learn
from simply listening...

there is always more to gain
by choosing to try...
there are so many people
who can empathize with the pain
and the suffering of someone else...
there are always going to be things
that happen to us that will shake
the ground beneath our feet,
that will disturb the equilibrium within our thoughts,
that will test us with the curse of uncertainty –
but everybody has to fight
every day to find the strength
to do what must be done,
to be able to feel what we have
always known we would have to feel,
to climb out of the darkness
where we can sometimes find ourselves,
and by following our heart
we can come to realize that
there are more things possible
than there are imaginable.

# Not Doing Christmas

Christmas is a wonderful time of the year…
Christmas can feel magical to children
and to people of all ages…
Christmas is about family and connection
and it is about sharing love and friendship;
however, for a lot of people,
more so now than ever,
Christmas is a time that they dread,
Christmas can feel "too much",
Christmas is a time that reminds
some people of what
and who they have lost.

Christmas decorations are lovely…
sending Christmas cards is sweet…
Christmas parties and gatherings are great,
and it is always good to let your hair down
and socialize with those whom you work with,
or perhaps those whom you may only see once a year;
but there are so many lonely people
who feel at their lowest during the festive period,
because they feel as if they have
forever lost the spirit that they once
had within them to be able to
enjoy the traditions
that have gone hand in hand
with Christmas and the New Year –
so much so that they wince
at the words "happy" and "merry"
that are used when someone
utters a Christmas wish.

Some people will have no choice
but to spend their time away from
those whom they love,
because coming together is,
for multiple reasons, particularly difficult...
for some people, Christmas
just does not feel the same as it used to
when times were better
and when there was more to look forward to.

Some children will make a list,
or write a letter to Father Christmas,
and hope that they get what they asked for;
however, every year, so many parents
know that there is no way
that they will be able to give
their children what they want,
but they will always endeavor
to give their children what they can –
and, more than anything,
love, happiness, and protection
is all that they really need.

For some people,
Christmas is when they can be themselves –
but, for some, Christmas can be
when people look into the faces
of family members and wish
that they could bring them
back full to health.

On Christmas day, multiple families
will open presents in the morning
and then in the afternoon
they will gather around a table
and enjoy a Christmas feast;
however, there will be those people
who on Christmas day will
not have one Christmas present to open
and will consider Christmas day
just like any other day.

There is always a reason for everything;
and while some people will make
the most of every second of
*"The most wonderful time of the year"*,
some people will not and will watch
the festive period pass without a fuss –
because, for personal reasons,
they choose to not do Christmas.

# Christmas Special

Some people, some things, some places
are special all year round –
but some people, some things, some places
feel more "Christmas Special"
because they can seem to symbolize
what makes Christmas the magical
time of the year that it can be.

Some songs, some films, some episodes
of some TV shows can only be
truly enjoyed when it is
the intended time of the year
that they were made to capture the feeling of –
whether that is the old favourite Christmas songs, like:
*"Christmas (Baby Please Come Home)* by Darlene Love,
*"Last Christmas"* by Wham!,
*"All I Want For Christmas Is You"* by Mariah Carey,
*"Fairytale of New York"* by The Pogues;
or festive movies, such as:
*"Home Alone," "It's A Wonderful Life,"*
*"Miracle on 34th Street," "Scrooge,"*
*"Elf,"* or *"Santa Claus: The Movie,"*
and many, many others –
which over time have become
staples of the festive experience,
and without them Christmas
just would not be Christmas.

Some pieces of clothing –
such as festive sweaters and Santa hats...
some food and drink –
such as turkey, stuffing, mince pies, mulled wine...
some decorations –
such as tinsel, baubles, and of course Christmas trees...
some weather conditions –
such as snow and ice –
seem to go with the time of the year
when Christmas is celebrated,
but might seem out of the ordinary
and an inconvenience at any other time
before or after the month of December.

Some things just sum up what Christmas is all about
and what it means to so many people all over the world...
some customs –
like decorating a real or an artificial tree,
or taking children to see Father Christmas –
are amazing and wonderful...
some of the rituals that people like to partake in –
like going to church, lighting a candle,
or saying a prayer for a dearly missed loved one –
are much needed for so many
to allow them to cope through
a sometimes difficult period
when so many people feel at their most vulnerable...
some of the most precious and joyous moments
you will witness all year
happen when people show how sharing,
how caring, and how selfless they can be –
and I think it is the way that people
communicate through their thoughts,
through their messages,
and through their actions,
which makes Christmas truly special.

# The True Journey

As one day becomes another...
as one year ends and another begins...
as time resets with an explosion of light and colour...
as people simultaneously celebrate what has come before
and hope for what awaits,
nobody can truly know how
they reached the point of crossroads
that they find themselves at, nor where the path
in front of them will take them;
however, each of us can rest assured
that the past influences the present,
just as the present dictates the future,
and all of our overlapping
and interwoven interactions
have a resonance that rings out
beyond the waves that are generated
at a moment of creation, at an explosion of rebirth,
at an instance of regeneration,
at a point when a threshold is traversed,
and, as a result, a door to a new world opens...
as we all continue to walk
where we have walked before,
as we all continue to share eye contact
with those whom we regularly see,
as we all continue to speak and hopefully be heard,
we all hope that the first time will not be the last time,
and that no matter what we have done
and how much time we have left on Earth,
it goes without saying that there is always more
for each and every one of us
to reach for, to experience, and to explore –
because the true journey has no end.

# Wild Card

There is always one...
there is always someone
who stands out from the crowd
because they refuse
to be like everyone else,
to think like everyone else,
to feel like everyone else –
even from those who
they consider their friends,
as well as from those of their family...
there is always someone extraordinary
who is capable of seeing what others cannot,
who can see a path where others see none,
who can work with what they have got
and make something seemingly out of nothing –
someone who is intrigued
by the mysteries of the unknown
and the uncertainties of life
that lie just beyond
the limits of their own eyes,
and who does not fear
where the universe will take them...

there is always something
that captures the imagination
and inspires the gift of the soul
of someone special to go out
and touch the energy
of the cosmic poetry around the world
that binds us all together,
and, in doing so, introduces them
to people along the way
who will influence them
to shine brighter than
the stars of the night-sky
and also inspire others
to follow their lead
with the commitment of a dart...
there is always someone
whose destiny is to go where
they know they need to venture –
even if doing so can't, at first, be understood;
because everybody has to do
what they have got to do,
and sometimes when people
have such a determination,
and carry such a spark
of change within their heart,
they can be considered
a "wild card".

# Nocturnal

Some people, some things,
some animals, some creatures
are nocturnal by nature –
they are more active after dark
and they thrive upon
the particular pursuits
that can only be undertaken
during the time of twilight.

Under the shroud of darkness
is when some individuals thrive
more so than they would
under the light of day,
because their instincts are
more attuned, accentuated,
and heightened when
the senses that they were born with
can be used to their maximum capability.

From owls to bats,
from badgers to whales,
from turtles to fireflies,
from people who work as firefighters
to people who work
in a bar or a nightclub –
so many prefer performing
and engaging in professional
and personal activities
when there is not as much
exposure as there is when
everything can be seen clearly.

As some people get older,
they find that they are unable
to stay up as late as they used
to be able to in their youth...
when some people have children
they find themselves having to
attend to those in their care
at times when it is not convenient –
including when others are
fast asleep and tucked up in their bed...
for some people, it is
what makes the night-time
so special and so magical
that which keeps them awake –
in particular, those who like to look up
to the sky and marvel at the wonders
that can be seen with the naked eye,
that have been the stuff
of dreams and fireside stories
since the first of humanity
discovered that it is
sometimes essential
to be nocturnal.

# The Lesson

It was always going to be this way...
it was always going to be me
finding myself back where it all began...
it was always going to be me
returning to the same place I started –
like restarting the performance of a play...
it was always going to be
a long and eventful road that I took
before I found myself, once again,
doing what I do, what I always do,
filled with memories and inspiration,
and, as always, without anything
that might resemble a plan.

It was always going to be me,
with an open notebook in front of me,
with my silver pen in my hand,
still with a hopeful smile on my face,
writing, thinking,
remembering, recalling,
watching, observing, looking
and finding more than might meet
the eye of everyone else but me...
it was always going to be me
back writing my poetry,
within my own bubble of imagination,
as the world, the universe,
the reality of life on this planet
carries on regardless around me.

It was always going to be me;
it was always going to be
who it was when things were
how they used to be;
it was always going to be
unlike what I, or anyone,
would ever have expected –
because everything that turned out
the way that it did
seems to have conformed
to a pattern that was
always meant to happen.

It was always going to be me
who would teach myself
that no matter how things
sometimes do change,
and how people sometimes
do take much-needed detours,
there is always a lesson to be learned
taught by time
and by our own inner shadow,
like only they can.

# Interlinked

Nothing and no one can prepare
for that moment of instant connection
that happens when two people
fall in love with one another...
so much can happen internally,
so much can be communicated
when two people see each other
for the first time...
nothing and no one can stop
the tidal wave of energy
that rises and then floods the air
around two people when they feel
as if their heart has been enlivened
and their soul has found
a match like no other...
so much can change when two people,
when two strangers,
realize that they have found
someone who they had no idea
they were searching for –
perhaps their entire life...

nothing and no one can feel,
nor could anyone else ever describe,
what two people who experience
this simultaneous,
and sometimes supernatural,
love goes through
when they find themselves
having to ask who the person
they have met is
and why they feel as if
they already know them, somehow...
so much makes sense,
so much is expressed,
so much goes through
a person's mind, and so fast,
that no one could ever truly
realise everything that happens
when the look of love that is shared
by two people, within the time
that it takes for them both to blink,
inextricably creates a bond between them
that forever makes them
consciously and unconsciously,
interlinked.

# Sometimes words are unnecessary

Sometimes, what we see,
what we hear, what we feel,
what we think, what we imagine
cannot always be put into words...
language is not always what we think it is...
sometimes, a picture is worth
more than a thousand words –
because an image can be what
reminds us of where we were,
with whom, and why;
a photograph taken when times were good
can be wonderful to see,
and yet bittersweet at the same time –
because pictures are like time capsules
of captured moments that are special,
because they are instances
that will never happen again...
in this world, at this time,
it is rare that even family members
gather together and celebrate with one another –
because, these days, so many people
live disparate existences from each other –
even though the physical distance
between them may not be as far
as they would like to believe...
sometimes, the most resonate sound
in the universe is silence –
because, even in the vacuum of space,
there lies an unheard secret
that speaks volumes about
why things are the way that they are,
and who people are
as well as who they think they are...

so many people feel out of place,
so many people feel out of touch,
so many people feel as if they have
nothing left to do and nothing left to offer –
until they have a moment
when they discover that they are not alone,
when they discover that they
have more to do,
when they discover that they might have,
perhaps, been seeing the world
through a shaded lens for far too long
and that when they see something spectacular:
a life-changing event –
like a sacred sunrise, or a sunset,
that opens their eyes and gives them
a vision of something that, perhaps,
they once thought was an impossibility;
however, in this universe
of improbability, and finality,
everything is meant to be –
but sometimes, when we search
for the words to describe something
or someone with the gift of poetry,
even a poet would agree that sometimes words are unnecessary.

# Multitude

This morning, I saw a distant light
shining from afar in the sky –
which was not the sun,
which was definitely not a plane,
and did not appear to be a drone;
however, the seemingly stationary light
that I saw from perhaps a mile away,
was enough to make me wonder
within my mind what it could be...
this morning, I also saw a white swan
and their cygnet swimming in a nearby pond;
and, as I watched the white swan
gracefully swim towards me,
almost immediately, I knew
that me seeing the swan,
and the swan seeing me,
was a sign of something significant,
a sign of something extraordinary
that has never been lost on me.

This morning, the sky is bright blue...
this morning, the light shines
unfiltered upon everything...
this morning, the chorus of caws
of the crows on the branches of their trees
are loud and distinctive,
just as the chirps of the robins
in the hedgerows are always
something sweet to hear
when they pay me a visit
as I proceed upon my path...

this morning, like every morning,
people carry out their daily rituals –
whether that is shopping,
reading, watching, or perhaps listening,
visiting one another, doing what they must,
as well as being there for those
who need help the most.

This morning, every morning, even as a child,
I am awoken with a mind of dreams,
thoughts, feelings, inspiration,
and, of course, poetry...
this morning, every morning,
looks the same as those that have come before –
but I always know that something is different,
I always know that something,
somehow, somewhere, has changed...
this morning, every morning,
I love being up early to see
the last lights of the night, the first light of the day,
and be witness to the moment
when silence becomes filled
with the sounds of a symphony...
this morning, every morning,
I know more than I am told
about life, the world, the universe,
and I instinctively feel the peaceful
harmony of the natural world
and the beginning of another wave
of that which binds everything –
both living and departed –
together beyond the limits
of the divine, eternal, and constant message
that is seen and interpreted
by everybody, everywhere, every day
in a multitude of ways.

# Through your fingers

I have always thought that we should
truly listen intently to the young,
because the young, especially children,
make a point to say what is on their mind;
I have always thought that the best thing about being young
is that you do not need to worry about anything,
nor think too much, and just live,
learn, look, sample, and have fun,
be adventurous without knowing it,
look in every direction –
not just forwards, or behind.

Every child sometimes forgets to look left and right
when they are crossing a road,
and sometimes they can walk away
by the skin of their teeth after a close encounter;
every child wants to be out and about with their friends –
whether it is a hot day of sun,
or a cold day of freezing snow;
every child is a not-so-secret natural explorer.

Children have no concept of time;
to a child the next day feels like a life-time away;
children have no thought of right or wrong, gift or crime;
to a child every day is like playing a game.

Every child attends a different school of thought
depending on where they live
and what they have been taught since the day they were born;
every child ultimately can only go on their own journey –

but the more a child has to choose
the more that they can feel torn;
and, to me, a child does need guidance
from those that they respect and trust,
but without too much of a push,
and letting them figure things out for themselves,
children always do find their feet.

A child from Africa can inspire the entire world
to think about others before themselves;
a group of friends from China can come together
from all different backgrounds
and dream of doing things, of going places,
and taking the rest of the world with them;
a little girl from Hawaii
can hear the voice of the Earth
when they listen to the sound
they find within a seashell;
a boy from Canada can one day be holding tightly
and looking down at his favourite toy,
and then one day years later in the future
take one simple thought that comes to him,
and realize that he could change the world
for every child and for all future children.

The life and the time of a child is precious,
and before you know it things get complicated,
and they can slowly start to lose their tender touch,
and they can worry about who they see in the mirror;
it is only natural to think
about why things are the way that they are,
but you just have to hold on to things
for as long as you possibly can –
because before you know it everything, slowly but surely,
falls through your fingers.

# Poetography

It's always strange looking back
at old photographs of yourself –
because we sometimes feel more comfortable
looking at pictures of other people, before ourselves…
it's a weird moment of reflection that occurs,
and a wave of deep introspection that engulfs us,
and helps to resurface memories and emotions
we once felt which are closely associated
with unforgettable thoughts that we had
and lived every second of,
that we dream about sometimes
when we are under the covers.

Looking at old photos,
reading back old diary entries,
experiences, and memories,
that we recorded, but forgot about –
looking and finding a piece of your past
always reminds us, and always reminds me,
instantly of where I was, who I was, what I was thinking,
and what life was showing me and guiding me to
with its many sign-posts;
reading a note that we once wrote,
and which ended up being left intact for us to find again one day,
now and forever reminds me again and again
that things happen for a reason and are meant to happen,
beyond any doubt.

I have been to many places,
and I love to go back to these same places on a different day,
at a different time, with a clutch of new colours
to my life and me in-toe.

Every day, everyone, and every place is different –
even though they, and we, may look and feel the same…
everything and everyone changes;
in fact, life dictates this for our, and its own, survival –
and that is the best way to think,
and that is the best way to go.

I look back often, because memories are important to me –
as are the people that I have met, all and everyone.

I take pictures of lots of things, and self-portraits of myself
every day to record and make a moment and a memory last
for as long as it can.

I look forward, and I look around me, every day
at the people in my life, and who I see
every day with my cyan-coloured eyes.

I write and capture as much as I can.

I am inspired, and I share every hello that makes me smile,
and every goodbye that makes me cry.

There are things that happen to us that are incredibly,
and intensely, personal, and they should be kept
and they should stay that way –
but I do believe that there are a great many things
that happen to all of us that must be shared,
because they too can light-up the life
and brighten the face of someone else
and make their day.

The world can seem like a smaller place now,
because we can share anything and everything
with literally millions of people simultaneously
all around the world in an instant;
the world feels more interconnected,
and our lives have become more interlaced,
and sewn-together like a patch-work quilt.

Ever since I was a child I have always felt
someone's presence before I saw them –
and ever since I went to school, and I started meeting
new kids and I started making friends,
I instantly realized the importance and the power,
the brilliance and the magic, of strangers,
friends, and unique once in a life-time memories.

Life begins, and passes you by in a flash
that can seem, when you look back,
to have all happened in the fraction of a second.

There is more that happens to us than we realize,
and there is more to see than could ever be seen –
by you or by me;
but I just enjoy and live every second
as if each and every one was my last on Earth,
and I love the gift of life and living free
so much that I have to write when I can
about the poetry in my heart, and all around me –
when I sit down and I share with as many people as I can
the exposure of the world that I see
in my *poetography*.

# Lifeline

We all need something to tie us to this world;
we all need someone to make us feel like we belong;
we all need someone to hold our hand from time to time
when the air goes cold;
we all need something to keep us listening to life's song.

One person can be the difference
between sadness and happiness;
one person can be the answer to a question
you have been asking all your life;
one person can be the difference between madness and calmness;
one person can be the star that guides you through every night.

One song can elevate existence to another level;
one voice can enhance the pleasures of the universe;
one melody can inspire you to rebel;
one word can free you from the pain of chaos
and stop your life from going in reverse.

We all need the sun;
we all need the moon;
we all need the touch of The One;
we all need the feeling of floating
high in the sky like a balloon.

One person's presence can send tingles down your spine;
one person's heart can make you feel alive;
one person's stare can make you feel divine;
one person's kiss can taste more sublime
than the most expensive glass of wine;
one person by your side when you need them,
who loves you as much as you love them,
can be a lifeline.

# The Little Things

Sitting in the park on a beautiful morning,
surrounded by light, life, and sound,
what I am doing feels life-reaffirming,
what I see is phenomenal, stunning, inspiring –
everything feels new, fresh, original, one of a kind,
never been seen before, bright,
beautiful, pulse-racing, exciting.

I don't want to leave.
I don't want it all to fade-away.
I don't want to take anything for granted.
I don't want this to just be another day.
It doesn't have to be, not if I don't want it to –
not as long as it is all about the me and the you.

Everyone walks through life at different speeds.
Everyone lives different lives with different needs.

In the city, I see people of all ages
and nationalities going about their day:
students coming to and from university,
smart-dressed men and women commuting to work,
children with a day off from school enjoying the sunshine
as they smile, run-around, and play;
kids discovering things with their parents,
parents discovering things about their kids –
from where I am, I see, and I embrace
what they will probably never remember or think about
until they get older:
those moments that define a child
and a parents relationship with each-other.

It is really nice to see
and to read the under-lying language
that only a member of the same family is fluent in and privy to –
those looks and expressions that only they know the meaning of,
which if you are an on-looker it is like a foreign-language,
or a code that you can never know.

You don't realize how precious time is
until you get older
and you see the people
and the places that you remember
change beyond recognition;
you don't realize how much you miss
until someone reminds you
of something that you shared together,
that meant so much to you at the time,
but unfortunately got filed-away
in the filing-cabinet of your memory –
now only a snap-shot of a moment,
which you never meant to ever forget,
but which fades over time like an old photograph –
that can be brought back to mind and life
with the help of only the smallest of reminders,
and enjoyed again, if it is a good memory
of a time in your life that you always want to put-away
and rediscover again over and over on a sunny day.

Every day I see someone I have never seen before –
even in places that I have been to a hundred times,
or down roads that I have walked
down more times than I can remember.

I see a new face –
I see the beginning, the middle,
or perhaps the last chapter of someone's story –
and every time I share eye-contact with a new person
I cannot help myself from wondering who they are,
who they will be;
I do not judge anyone by how they appear,
because to everyone –
even those who you think you know –
there is always more to see.

I cherish the little things about people and about life…
I adore the moments that people
freely throw-away without a second thought
that tell you about them –
a story that they recite to themselves
when they fall asleep at night.

Sitting seemingly alone on a bench, on a hill,
in a park of untouched green grass,
looking out, looking up, looking within,
I have a moment of ponderance,
and in silence I think about the story that I am writing,
the legacy that I am leaving;
why I am who I am;
why the people and the things
that I care so much about
mean so much to me;
why, even though I have no one
beside me, I am not alone –
what that means, and why that
is so important to remember.

# Snowman's Paradise

Snowflakes swirl, fly, and dance, in the air,
as they slowly descend to the already white-covered floor –
billions of intricate and perfect frozen tears
dusting and blanketing the world before me.

It is like standing in the middle of a snow-globe.

No one can see anything in front of them...
everyone just jeeps going as best, as fast,
and as cautiously, as they can –
not letting the weather keep them in one place,
not even this unrelenting snowfall.

Seeing familiar landmarks veiled below frozen fields
that makes everything look
indistinguishable from everything else,
a new world reveals itself, a new light shines,
a new beauty arises,
the sky becomes the Earth, the Earth becomes the sky;
the sun is obscured from view, all is bright,
and suddenly everyday things that you may sometimes miss
start to catch your eye.

A red British postbox has never looked more amazing
and glowing than against a white backdrop;
roads and motorways have never seemed more ghostly,
nor more other-worldly, than when you drive down them
in the middle of a blizzard,
when you are relying on the lights of the vehicles
in front of you to save you from coming to a sudden,
immediate, and perhaps costly stop.

Walking on what you cannot see,
walking on something that you have
to constantly reteach yourself
how to walk on with every step,
makes you think more about your surroundings,
it forces you to not take anything for granted,
and to expect the unexpected –
it doesn't take much to take a false step in the snow below
and seconds later to find yourself in a skid.

In this weather you need to wrap-up warm,
keep on the move, to stay dry,
to make the most of every shelter
and cover that you come across…
don't rush to wherever you are going,
give yourself time; stay inside –
the snow can seem like a disruption
if you have got somewhere to go;
but you cannot not appreciate its beauty, its magic,
its gift of contemplation –
because nothing else opens your eyes to the world wider.

Looking at the world,
staring at the white cloud-covered sky,
at the snow-carpeted ground,
and at the bare branches of the trees,
while wearing the biggest
and the warmest coat that I could find
to protect me from the cold and the ice –
I look at where I am standing,
I look at the landscape that nature is remaking,
and I smile to myself at the thought that,
as things stand right now,
this must be the most perfect
winter wonderland that I have ever seen,
and it would be the most sublime snowman's paradise.

# Solo

I am alone.
I am the protector and the keeper of a sacred light.
I cannot let this beacon go out.
I must continue to shine.
Just as the stars must continue to burn,
distant, constant, and white.

The ocean is never still,
however people continue to cross it –
no matter its unpredictability;
a heart never stops beating –
however, no matter how much
fortification you have around it,
you should treat it as a miracle,
and marvel at every beat
as if it were your last;
and cherish every breath like a flame
that dances between life and infinity.

I feel a dream-wave come over me,
and then immediately wash me out to sea
to the realm of the dream-maker:
I dream that I am on a boat traversing through an icy sea,
as I stare up at the stars above me in the sky
from the bow of an unstoppable and mighty ice-breaker.

I am awoken again by a flash of lightning
and a clap of thunder;
but the sky and the sea are calm,
clear, and golden, so far –

looking out now you could so easily
mistake what you see for a dream,
because the vista of the vast water
is more akin visually right now
to a beautiful sunrise landscape on Mars.

I pass from day into night so easily.
I welcome the arrival of the moon,
just as I cherish the rise of the sun.
I can go from walking under the stars in the dark,
to hearing and seeing every detail of day life
while on a morning run.

When I see the light of others go out around me,
I mourn their passing as if I were
mourning the loss of something inside of me –
that for every hour that passes
continues to mean something deeper.

I cherish the memory and the light of others,
just as I cherish the light within me
that shines for all the world to see –
because I am a dreamer,
because I am a guardian of hope,
because I am a lighthouse keeper.

# Eclipse

The Sun is shining brightly in the sky...
the birds are singing and flying above in the air...
there isn't a cloud or a frown to be found anywhere –
it is as if it were a normal, beautiful, day,
when everything around everyone
can easily be understood and quantified;
and then, slowly, darkness sweeps over the world
and bathes all in shadow: as a planet, a moon, and a star,
come into perfect alignment together,
and our greatest inspirations in our sky put on a show.

Within a matter of a few seconds,
day has seemingly become night, all eyes look above to the sky
where a phenomenon of nature is taking place:
our Sun's light has momentarily been eclipsed –
leaving only a faint golden halo to be seen,
where minutes ago it was shining epically,
blindingly, boldly, and brightly.

What was being witnessed now by all,
under this veil of magical solar and lunar synchronicity,
was strangely and instantly emotional for myself
and for everyone around me.

I felt humble, and small –
but also blessed, content, overwhelmed,
and elevated, somehow,
as if I were now ten feet tall.

For the briefest of seconds,
everyone was transfixed
by the exact same thing,
at the exact same time,
and it felt like we were in the midst
of something incredibly special:
something that no one on Earth had a part to play in,
but which they were intended to have witnessed –
something wholly divine.

Then, a burst of unbelievable light
exploded on the left-hand-side of the ring
and separated the sun and the moon from their union…
sunlight washed over the world again like a wave,
and revealed Earth –
humanities home,
that we sometimes take for granted –
to be the perfection that we have
been looking for all our lives:
the enigma that requires no solution.

The moon slowly fades beyond our sight, for now,
and the sun seems bigger, brighter,
as if it had been remade
behind the silhouette of the moon,
somehow.

People continued to look at the sun
in almost disbelief at what they had seen
for a few minutes more sometime after,
before returning to whatever it was
that they were doing before –
some were still in-awe of the spectacle,
some returned to work without hesitation,
and some people celebrated their joy
at having shared such an experience together
by kissing each-other on the lips.

I stood with my hands behind my back,
with my eyes closed,
hypnotised long-after
by the meaning of the moments
of darkness and light –
still with the thoughts in my mind
that were brought to life
by the gift of the eclipse.

# The Dandelion Universe

A dandelion head bobbing in the breeze –
a common sight to those who
regularly venture-out into nature,
and the appearance of which,
I have to say, always puts me at ease –
is incredibly inspiring to me;
because, even though it is small in stature,
it reminds me of something greater.

Looking at the head of a dandelion, to me,
is like looking at a physical
capture of the spark, the seed,
the beginning and the evolution of the universe;
looking at a dandelion,
and holding a head in my hands,
evokes a sense of the delicacy
of life on Earth, and beyond –
on our planet, in our seas,
in the skies of distant planets,
in the constant creation
and destruction of distant lands.

When you look at a dandelion,
you would think that
you are looking at an explosion
that has been frozen in time –
that is because you are,
and to me that is what is the most sublime.

Dandelions –
like galaxies, maybe even universes –
come in many different stages and sizes,
and within their biology dandelions
have many beneficial, necessary,
and life-sustaining, surprises.

When you see the seeds
of a dandelion dispersing
and being blown into the wind –
the sight and the spectacle is beautiful to see,
but witnessing it happen
can also make your heart sink;
however, that is the universe in the smallest
and in the most simplest of examples:
think of the universe as a dandelion in a field
and you will understand that what we see,
and what we believe we know about life,
are nothing but insights, spoilers, and samples.

A dandelion, in all its forms,
is an amazing sight,
and its seeds are a reminder to me
that creation goes on
like the stars of the night sky –
expanding outwards, and never going in reverse –
and that is why I believe that if
we are looking to call the cosmos a name,
we should seriously consider
calling all of creation
"The Dandelion Universe".

# X

Xylophone voices echo through the darkness;
tones of truth, vibrations of variables –
perfection professed.

The answer to a question:
this is why you are here –
this is why you and everyone live, die,
and exist on this precious sphere.

Over the millennia of our evolution
humanity has taught itself to divide, and to fear;
however, in doing so it has inspired
the entire species to learn and understand
that things are not always as they first appear.

The unspoken answer, and the,
as yet, unrealized meaning of our makeup –
the answer that can be found
within at the same time we are looking up;
the answer that is discovered, named,
rediscovered, generation-after-generation:
that we all have a phenomenal facet,
will, and a capacity to excel
and to overcome any limitation.

The ability of humanity to have the power
to write the destiny of all life on planet Earth
has been a part of us all since our primordial birth,
and one day soon I have hope
that we will all use the gifts of our birthright,
and build what life projects:
a meaning to live that is enlightening as it is complex.

# The Golden Rule

If there is one rule to life
that I believe in, that I live by,
that I have seen
the results of time after time,
it would have to be the so-called
*"The Golden Rule"* –
the same principle as that which
was spoken by Jesus in his
Sermon on the Mount in The Bible –
essentially: *"Do unto others
as you would have them do unto you"*;
and, to me, *"The Golden Rule"* is important
because it simply explains
why we should be selfless,
and why we should all think
about others first before ourselves –
and if you believe in karma
then you will know that actions
have consequences,
and what we do comes back to us;
and that is why we should
all always be mindful
of what we put out into the world.

# The World of My Stories

A person's life is filled with different characters;
a person's world is filled with many horizons;
a person's life can be organized and thought of
as like a book of interconnected chapters;
a person's view of the world changes over time
as they live, experience, and grow older –
and, from my perspective, I am so glad
for the life that I have had and still have,
because my life is a trove of golden-moments
and a limitless garden of inspirational memories
and musings that thrive and infuse
the palette of my writing,
because there is so much in abundance.
Just as every solar-system has a star at its centre,
the world of my poetry and stories too has a sun
that it revolves around and gives it gravity
and keeps it spinning;
just as every planet has a combination of gases
that make up its atmosphere,
the world where my ideas are born from
has all that is needed to keep my internal world
alive and its creations breathing, living, and evolving.
Worlds are built over time
and of many components and ingredients;
over a life-time, and while writing a story,
there is a constant preoccupation
to find truth, sense, and balance;
some worlds can be vast, and some worlds can be small –
expanding and contracting, depending on a person's
state of mind and their environment;
over time we all collect many things in many ways –

however, it isn't until you start thinking about
writing a story of your own that you realize
that even the smallest of things
can be among that which is the most important.
Usually, the idea for a new story comes to me like a dream;
for the most part, what a story will be about,
when I am writing one, all depends and is centered
upon something I have felt, or something I have seen;
when I first begin writing a story
it is like I am learning to walk again
and not worrying too much about or counting my steps;
when I get into a story and I have fully found my footing
and I know where my story is going,
it is then that I race towards its ending
without fear of losing my breath.
I love writing stories –
however, to me, writing a story
is like running a marathon;
to me writing poetry is like going on a sprint
through the green and blue world of my head –
and it is while writing poetry
that I get to let my imagination go wild,
and I get to sometimes write what I see;
writing a story is like creating and making
something that to you is a labour of time and love.
I am a writer, and more than anything I love to write –
however, sometimes I feel like
there could never be enough words
to describe what I see when I look within;
but my constant wish is to find a way
to show people what lies inside me
and take them on a tour
around the world of my stories.

# Kindred Spirits

When you know you have found a kindred spirit –
someone who likes the same things as you,
someone who speaks the same language as you,
someone who knows a part of you that no others do,
nor could ever understand –
the recognition is almost instant...
when you meet someone
and from the moment that you
share something about yourself with them –
that perhaps defines the most
important part of what makes you –
you know that what you say
will mean more to them
than it might to someone
whose interests are more
divergent from yours...
when you have a shared experience
with people whom you may have only known
for a relatively short amount of time –
but who you feel already have an instinct
about something that will always
remain a fundamental principle
that keeps alive the spark of hope within you –
then you will naturally gravitate back to them
time and time again –
because each and every one of us
never stop looking for something
or for someone who gets
why we are the way that we are
and why we do what we do...

when you can communicate
an entire universe of stories, characters, adventure,
and the universal phenomenon that something has become,
with a simple, yet infinitely powerful,
phrase, a gesture, a look
that can encapsulate and symbolize
why it is as special as people believe it to be,
then you know that what you
and many others have in common
is worth every second that you have put into it...
when you find joy in the art
of becoming someone else –
just like an actor who transitions
and transforms themselves into a character –
you know that what comes with
that overwhelming feeling of happiness
is a tangible connection
with others that makes you feel seen
and not judged in any way,
and that experience can mean
so much to so many people
more that they could say...
when you come to believe
that there is no limit to what you can achieve
as long as you hold on to what empowers you,
like an enduring gift –
and then you recognize the same look in the eye
of others who also know
that they have a responsibility
to do something with
that which continuously gives them
the same enlightened lift –
that is when you know
you have found a fellow
kindred spirit.

# Let There Be Poetry

In the beginning,
there was something –
there always is;
however, then something else happened:
an explosion of energy and light,
and, in an instant, poetry
came into existence and continued
to create and reinvent itself,
over and over again,
until it eventually evolved into
life, sounds, images,
music, words, language,
vast connections that span
the multiverse of universes
and realities that currently exist, and beyond –
and there is no sign of it stopping any time soon.

Poetry has always been there…
poetry is always there in every moment,
and poetry will always be there
waiting to be seen, recorded,
recounted, and shared...
poetry is not just words –
poetry is like a fire
that burns without end...
poetry lies within the heart
of every person on Earth...
poetry has been there
within the dreams of everyone
who has ever lived
since the moment of their birth.

Since I first discovered poetry,
since I wrote my first poem,
since I first discovered that
becoming a poet and writing
my own poetry was my destiny,
since I started and I couldn't stop myself
from being inspired by everything and everybody,
I have been seeing the world
through the prism of infinite possibilities...
since I first started sharing
what I saw, what I heard,
what I felt, what means the most to me –
when I was gifted that first moment
of poetic serenity and clarity –
I have believed in the concept of causality,
I have believed that everything happens for a reason,
because it has to,
because it is meant to,
and when it comes to finding an explanation
as to why things happen in life
I have always believed in the old saying,
*"Whatever will be... will be"* –
which is why I have always believed
there is always an answer for everything,
and that even in the darkest of times,
or during the brightest of days,
things have a way of showing us just how much of life
is beyond our control and full of surprises,
but life also has an innate design to it that is meant to repeat;
so, just as a long time ago
a phrase was uttered that made the first light shine
across the cosmos, I say: "let there be poetry" –
so that people everywhere
may know what it means to be free
to be who they are supposed to be.

# What Comes Naturally

When we are young
we invariably tend to try
many different things –
usually all at once –
until we are observed to be
gravitating to something in particular
more often than the other things
that have repeatedly occupied our attention –
whether that is a person,
a song, a story, a film,
or perhaps a character in a TV show that,
for whatever reason, keeps us
coming back for more...
as we get older, we are found
to be engaged in an activity
that we had done over and over again –
because whatever we find enjoyment in doing
gives us the gift of something
we cannot get from anywhere else,
nor from anyone else...
while growing up, we are all
constantly being influenced
by those around us to participate
in something that other people
also like to do –
but, most of the time,
what we really want to do
is to be able to choose
the pursuit and the path
that to us is unparalleled by anything
that anybody else might recommend...

when we discover that
we have the freedom to be,
to do, and to go wherever we want,
we always choose the first thing
that comes to our mind –
but, sometimes,
the conviction necessary
to transform us into who we want to be,
and to take us where we want to be,
needs to be inspired by something,
or someone else,
that acts like a spark that ultimately
leads to a raging fire...
when we eventually find out
who and what we want to be,
sometimes we can believe
that perhaps time has run out
and the opportunity to do
what we have always wanted to do
has long since passed –
because we let other things
get in the way of our dreams;
but the truth is that there really is
no time like the present
to make a life-long wish come true,
because no matter when
you start something new
you instantly discover
that the most important things in life
are those that come naturally.

# Pilgrimage

We all know what it is like
to have the image of a person,
a place, or something in particular,
within our mind, that gifts us,
every time we think of them,
with a surge of energy,
enthusiasm, and power...
we all know what it is like
to be drawn to someone,
to somewhere, to something,
as if we were being pulled
towards them by a force like that of gravity,
to which we can believe
we are destined to go
so that something inside us
can be unlocked by using
them as if they were a key...
we all know the feeling of anticipation
that rises within us
when we start to get this instinct
that the time when we will one day
fulfil the promise of serendipity,
and make a dream come true,
and the voice of that which calls us
towards them, gets steadily louder...
we all know what it feels like
to be on a journey somewhere –
both familiar and unfamiliar –
and what it means to us
to return to somewhere special,
as well as to see something,
somewhere, that for so long
has seemed out of reach...

we all know what it takes
to do something that
we have never done before –
and sometimes we have to,
somehow, change how we think
about something in order
to be able to fully integrate
and interact with where we
find ourselves and with whom
we find ourselves with...
we all know what it is like to have
heroes whom we look up to
and whom we seek out for guidance
about what we should do
and perhaps where we should go next –
because every day everybody
is on a journey towards
something that will always
continue to be both tangible,
and yet far away –
because even when we finally
make it somewhere we have always wanted to go,
or after we finally meet someone
who we have always wanted to meet,
what matters is what happens afterwards
and as a result of the steps
that we all have to take
on our own individual and personal,
life-long and meaningful,
pilgrimages.

# Someone To Talk To

When we are young,
we are told that we can do anything,
we are told that we can go anywhere,
and we are told that we can be
who and what we want to be,
as long as we work hard
and don't give up, no matter what;
but, as we grow older, as we experience
more of what life is all about,
we all discover that there are times
when we need others to help us –
because sometimes we can't
make it through life alone.

Everybody in their life
lives through times of joy,
love, beauty, optimism –
when there are times to be
happy and hopeful;
but, unfortunately, instances
and experiences can be like
water through someone's fingers,
and, ultimately, over time,
everything and everyone
becomes a memory
that you must hold on to
a fragment of to allow
them to be preserved
in a meaningful
and timeless way.

Everything changes...
everyone changes...
people lose their lives...
people lose their jobs...
people lose someone who
meant the world to them...
people find themselves in a crisis
from which they cannot see a way out of...
people lose hope –
and when that happens,
no matter who a person is, was,
what they were, and what they had,
everybody longs for and reaches to
those who have been there for them
in the past when they needed them;
however, as things change,
as people change,
so too do the relationships
between people –
but, sometimes, all that everyone needs
is the opportunity to speak,
to be heard, and, most importantly,
to be listened to and understood –
and, in this life, the older you get
the more that you realise that
you don't need much more
than someone who you can trust
and the one person in the world
you would choose when you need
someone to talk to.

# From One to Another

It is always great to be able
to share what you know
about something that
you have learned a lot about
with friends, with family,
and with people who share
the same interests as you –
but whenever you meet
someone who,
from the moment that you met them,
seems to be talking the same language
that, for so long, you were led to believe
that only you could communicate in
and understand,
then there is always
a wave of energy
that touches you...
no matter how well and how long
someone may have known you,
it is only those who have
walked the same path as you,
it is only those who have had
similar experiences as you,
it is only those who have been born
with a similar gift as you –
whatever that may be –
who can truly understand you,
and why and how
you do what you do.

When you are with someone
who, like you, can see order
where others only see chaos...
when you are with someone
who, like you, enjoys looking within –
while others only look outwards...
when you are with someone
who, like you, has a reason for
why they invest so much of their time
connected to something that matters to them,
every interaction can feel so effortless –
while, when you are with others
who do not share the same
passion about something,
it can be hard to put into words
to someone who does not
speak the same way as you do,
who does feel the same way
about things as you do,
who does not wish for
the same things as you do,
why, when we find ourselves
somewhere in particular,
everything feels so natural.

There is a reason why like-minded
people attend conferences
and conventions that revolve around
a common endeavour or pastime...
there is a reason why some stereotypes are true
and why certain characteristics
about certain types of people do recur...
there is a reason why certain people –
from magicians to comedians,
from actors to writers,
from gardeners to aficionados
who enjoy doing many different
individual and collaborative activities –
gather together and meet
without the feeling of guilt
that can stir within you, sometimes,
when you reveal to someone
something that you take pleasure in doing,
as if you have committed a crime...
there is a reason why
we all secretly seek out others
who we know will immediately understand
something fundamental about us
from the instant that our paths cross –
because nothing feels more refreshing
than conversing with someone
when whatever you say to each other
every word uttered
feels like the steps of a sprint
that rapidly transitions
from one to another.

# Flow State

I have always compared
how I feel when I am writing
and I am inspired
with someone turning on a tap...
I have always thought
of the experience that I have
when I am creating something
with someone walking
or running down a path...
I have always felt as if
I am being connected
to something else while writing –
as if I am communicating,
sharing, and receiving a message,
or gaining a new insight
as a result of my consciousness
swimming, diving, feeling
and interpreting the energy
of an ocean of poetry around me
that brings to the surface
something that I did not know was within me...
I have always been able to sit
in silence and feel my thoughts
drift away –
but while listening to music
I have also had the experience
of feeling as if my mind were
generating the landmasses
of a whole new world
of endless possibilities...

I have always known that there were other realities
beyond the ones that most people
see and are familiar with,
since I was a child and I started
to silently speculate and continue
the stories of characters
others believed had come to an end...
I have always known
that I had a gift that I was meant
to share with others
that was too powerful to be kept hidden
from my family and my friends...
I have always been someone
who honestly felt recharged
by feeling the touch of the sun
upon my skin, as if I were
a human solar-panel connected
to a renewable battery...
I have always been someone who loved to read –
but I had no idea that I would
fall in love with being a writer
until I wrote that first poem of poetry...
I have always been able to slip in
and slip out of a moment of time
and explore many different
routes to where I need to get to
within a slip-second,
but also be inclined
to adapt to what I find and be influenced
by whom I find along the way...
I have always been able to let go of what I know
and see many different sides to something,
and sometimes someone –
especially when I am in my
"flow state".

# Behind The Scenes

Behind the curtain of a stage,
below the surface of an ocean,
underneath the seemingly
calm veneer of someone's smile –
there always lies
more than meets the eye...
when you look up
at a star in the night sky
it looks so peaceful –
but if you were to actually see
the same star up-close,
instead of far away,
then you would see
a burning sphere of energy
that looks more chaotic and dynamic
than it does from a distance
against the dark backdrop of space
upon which it shines.

A lot of planning and preparation
goes into making something
look so seamless and easy...
a lot of rehearsing goes into helping
a company of people know
what to do and when...
a lot of hours goes into making
something transition into being real,
after so long of just being a dream...

a lot of practice goes into
the performance of a lifetime –
even the most naturally talented
musician, singer, artist, or athlete
has to put everything into what they do,
even if that means having to forego
doing what others do
because they have to focus
all their time and attention
on being their best.

Like everything that matters
to people in life,
that from the outside seems simple,
so much always has to happen,
so much is always happening,
so many things have to
synchronize with one another
in order for an experience
to be considered special and magical –
and one of the things that is essential
is to constantly have faith and to believe,
because an infinite number of things
than could ever be known
have to happen
for everything to happen,
every moment of every day,
everywhere,
behind the scenes.

# Home Movies

Ever since I was young,
capturing moments of time
with a camera has been important
to me and to my family –
especially to my amazing Dad:
who used to record home movies
of us when we used to go on family holidays
to Orlando, Florida,
in the United States of America...
when I was a boy,
my Dad used to take photos of us
whenever we would go somewhere together –
because to my Dad photographs
were like memories,
and because my Dad loved his family
and he loved sharing his life
with his adoring wife and his children
whenever he would look back upon
the joyous instances that he had captured
you could see in his eyes
what every second with us
meant to him.

Children grow up so fast...
families change –
especially when things happen
that are out of their control...
no matter how old someone is
everybody always
daydreams of the past...

as we all move from place to place,
and as we all meet new people,
we all adapt and to wherever we are
and we all find ourselves
undertaking new roles –
and there are always things
that we hold on to
which always give us
a jolt of nostalgia
every time we hold them again:
perhaps something that we had
forgotten about that feels like
the piece of a puzzle
which reminds us of something
that once meant the world to us.

Family photos are both wonderful,
and yet bittersweet, reminders
of who we were, where we were,
and with whom, once upon a time,
when things were different...
memorable songs are great to hear again –
but whenever you hear a certain song
playing somewhere, at some time,
everybody always has
an emotional reaction,
and sometimes a particular song
can make you think of someone
you have lost but also someone
whose soul still feels
close enough to touch.

The stories of things and people
often outlast and endure
beyond those who they are about,
because everybody loves
to be entertained
by the exploits and the adventures
of someone whose memory
and spirit is indelible
and sometimes tangible –
and there are times when
the image of something, or someone,
can say even more than
a thousand words about them could,
especially when someone who
is a natural storyteller shows
what and who meant the most to them
through whom they chose
to record and to remember
whenever they picked up a camera
and captured in every second
of their home movies.

# Apricity

I have always been able to feel
and appreciate the energy
that surrounds me...
I have always been able to
subconsciously see
the spectrum of colour
that everything and everyone radiates...
I have always been able to hear
the music of the spheres –
the cosmic symphony
that the stars and planets of the universe
play every instant of every day
as members of the eternal orchestra...
I have always been able to assimilate
the knowledge of someone,
something, or somewhere
simply by reaching out
and touching the ever-present spirit
that everyone and everything
emanates and leaves behind them
like some kind of echo of their aura...
I have always been a believer
in the importance of obligation –
to the people who matter to us,
as well as to the place where we call home...
I have always been a dreamer
and someone with an imagination
that daily refreshes itself
with new hopes and dreams
for the future...

I have always been someone
who has always felt connected
to something greater than myself –
which is probably why,
even when I am seemingly by myself,
I never feel alone,
and I always feel love...
I have always been someone
with an instinct that allows me
to be able to look
and listen to someone
and instantly know what mechanism
drives their internal desires...
I have always been someone
who has been able to take a walk
on a summer's day,
or stop and look up to the sky above
on a winter's afternoon,
and feel instantly inspired,
revitalised, and uplifted by the
apricity of every moment –
as if I am being remade every time
by the extraordinary feeling
of the sun upon my skin.

# The Great Communicator

Even from a young age,
everybody finds a way
to communicate with others
what they want and what they need...
from children to adults,
everybody has their own particular way
to indicate what colours they use
to paint the world of their dreams...
growing up, everybody discovers
that they have strengths that help them
interact with the world –
but now, more than ever,
people have gotten used to
interacting with others anonymously
and they can easily transition
from who they are, what they say,
and how they are perceived in real life,
to who they want to be,
what they want to say,
and how they want to be seen virtually.

Talking and communicating with others
is an art that does not come
as naturally to some
as it does to others...
it is always miraculous
to witness a child watch, listen, learn,
and then, over time, repeat
and even mimic what they have heard
and what they have seen –

and the more people
that they spend time around
and the more time that they spend
speaking and acting without thinking
then you get to see
who they are slowly becoming,
what they like to spend their time doing,
and perhaps what aspects
of their young personality
will become more defined
as they get older.

Not everyone grows up
having people around them
who see and immediately recognise
that they are special and gifted...
some children have parents
who immediately want to mould them
into becoming another version of them –
instead of letting their child
find their own feet, find their own language,
and find out who they are supposed to be –
which is why some children defy
the wishes of their elders
and gravitate towards those
who also share the same instinct
to insight chaos instead of maintaining order...
everybody makes mistakes
throughout their lives,
and everybody sometimes
says the wrong thing –

even though it seemed like
the right thing to say at a particular time;
but who would any of us be
if we did have an opportunity
to readjust ourselves after
becoming side-tracked by something
that we formed a strong relationship with...
some people seem to have such
an innate and natural ability
to be able to do something
that it can almost seem as if
they were always meant to be
who they have grown to become;
however, each of us –
no matter how old we are –
daily have to realign ourselves
to the direction that we know
we must travel towards,
but sometimes all that people need
to guide them is an internal compass
that allows them to always find
where their "True North" lies
so that they can have
something to anchor them,
while they are able to seek out
the sometimes diverse realities
that are able to exist within the same world,
as well as finding joy in the act
of walking out upon a stage
that many others have done so before,
and finding something
that was left for them as a gift of
"The Great Communicator".

# Brum

I love walking around this city...
I live walking from one side to the other –
from the China Town on the East side
to the Jewelry Quarter on the West Side –
and exploring all the sights and sounds
that make this bustling city
the city of inclusion that it is,
that has waiting around every corner
a wealth of inspiration
to fuel the imagination
and drive the pen of any poet,
and which has so many mesmerizing murals
of artistic expression to be found
painted upon so many of its walls.

There are diamonds of beauty
to be found in even the darkest
of alleyways and streets...
there are towers of metal and glass
standing alongside old brown brick
buildings that used to house
so many renowned staples of
manufacture and innovation
in many different and varied forms –
from transport to metallurgy –
that originated from the heart
of this great country
and to this day still drive
the engine of this country.

There are places of natural beauty...
there are places of sacredness...
there are landmarks that define this city
which every visitor is advised to see,
document, and share that cannot be found anywhere else –
for example: the bronze statue of
"The Birmingham Bull" that stands outside
one of the entrances to the Bullring Shopping Centre,
the sprawling canal system,
the world-renowned Birmingham
Indoor and Outdoor Markets,
as well as all the other quintessential
gifts that the city of Birmingham
adds to the British people's diverse mixture of history,
culture, languages, accents, and individuality.

Birmingham has been the birthplace
of many public figures who have risen
to a state of recognition over the years...
ever since it was founded
Birmingham's many city streets have been where all kinds
of people have entered the public imagination
and have made a name for themselves...
Birmingham has always boasted
having several unique individuals
who have never been afraid to make their
uniquely sounding voice be heard
far and wide, morning, noon, and night –
and every day I have witnessed
the people, and the different quarters
of this city, sparkle, shine,
emanate, and embody what
puts the "Great" in Great Britain –
the city that I know and
I which have walked many miles around:
the city of Birmingham.

# Repetition

Everybody occasionally repeats themselves...
everybody eventually discovers
that they are a part of a cycle...
everybody returns to the same place
over and over again,
but every time everybody
finds themselves back
where they are used to being
they are always different –
even though where they are
may look exactly the same
and as if nothing has changed...
everybody sometimes catches
a glimpse of their own reflection
and they are taken aback
by the almost invisible
scars that they see –
and not just the ones
that might be present upon their face...
everybody remembers everything –
even though they may have
led themselves, and others,
to believe that some of things
that may have happened
had been forgotten...
everybody always reveals more
about who they are –
especially the more
that they are observed trying,
and sometimes failing,
to break the bad habits
that they are known for;

however, with time, with experience,
with hindsight, everybody always gains
the wisdom that they need
to sever the chain of past behaviours
and forge new links
that will enable the revelation
of new possibilities and realities
that might not have been
thought possible before...
everybody sometimes feels
as if they are within
the event horizon of a black hole,
and stuck in an infinite revolution –
like an album being played,
and then replayed, on a loop;
but the truth is, no matter what
seemingly never-ending groove
you think you are stuck in,
everybody can always escape any trap
by simply realising where they are
and what they have been doing,
and then choosing to change
and to perhaps leap into the vortex
of what they cannot know –
and only then can everybody feel
the true sensation of release
that comes with the end
of something that someone may
have hoped and prayed for a long time
they could stop repeating.

# Walking on Air

When you fall in love with someone,
you become weak,
you become vulnerable,
you become different...
when you fall in love with someone,
you lose your identity –
because another is rising
to take its place...
when you fall in love with someone,
sometimes you get the feeling
that you both once shared something
a long time ago –
perhaps in a previous life,
as seen through a filtered lens...
when you fall in love with someone,
everything around you feels blurred
in comparison to who now occupies
what you see and who you think about
all hours of the day...
when you fall in love with someone,
you instantly believe
that nothing and no one
could ever compare to them...
when you fall in love with someone,
you can't wait to spend every moment
in their presence and be hypnotized
by their entrancing glare...

when you fall in love with someone,
it almost feels as if
this time is the first time
all over again...
when you fall in love with someone,
gravity itself does not feel
as strong, nor as important
as it should –
because the force,
the energy,
the power of love
that songs and poetry
have been full of
since the first poets
found a way to capture
the transformative
journey into the unknown
that our soul takes
when we all experience
the recurring sensation
of getting closer
to the stars of the sky
than to the ground
below our feet –
because we feel as if
we are levitating
and walking
on air.

# There is no tomorrow

It is good to dream,
and it is good to be a dreamer...
it is good to believe,
and it is good to be a believer...
it is good to send out a message of hope
into the universe without knowing
if you will ever receive a reply...
it is good to make a list of things
you want to do and places
you want to visit before you can't...
we all wish that some things
could be different and that we could
somehow go back and change what happened;
however, we are not meant
to have the power of a god,
we are not meant to live beyond
the last day of our destined journey,
we are not meant to know everything –
but each and every one of us,
right this second, have something
that we have in common:
an opportunity to choose
where we will go next, why, and how...
the past is fixed, indelible,
and what happened before is what it is...
the present is where we find ourselves now –
and everybody knows that
there is something important that they want to do,
there is somewhere that they want to be,
and, usually, it is doing something else
and being somewhere else
than where they are...

the future does not exist until it does –
and, for most people, the future
is so far away and so elusive
that they do not realise
they have arrived there
until they take a look around
and see how much things
and people have changed...
every day we are alive,
we travelling into the world to come –
and as we get older
each day seems to pass us by faster and faster,
as if we have all unwittingly
always be the participants within a race...
in life, we all lose more than we gain;
but it is over the course of our life
that we get to experience
and witness moments like no other,
and there is no better time
than today, and right away,
to do what you want to do,
to go where you want to go,
and to be with whoever
wants to be with you –
because, when it comes to
making a choice that will
effect your life forever,
the present is all that matters,
because there is no tomorrow.

# The Pathfinder

When we all start down
upon a new path
no one can know exactly
where it will lead –
nor who they will meet along the way...
when we all begin again
in our attempt to find where
we are meant to be and with whom,
no one can know how much
of who they are will remain –
nor what about them will ultimately change.

I have been walking down
a path of poetry for as long
as I can remember...
I have been running
through a forest of imagination
since I was a child...
I have been listening to the sounds of nature
for as long as I have been able to hear...
I have been seeing
the infinite possibilities
of life and the universe
since my mind was opened wide
after asking questions
and being given answers
that brought to life my love
of the mysterious of the unknown
that, to this day, still continue
to energize my thoughts
like the waves of light and colour
that can be seen while witnessing
the Northern Lights.

Once I have been somewhere,
I never forget where I have been
nor what I have seen...
once I have been somewhere,
I never forget how to return there –
because I have always had this innate gift
to be able to create a map
of places within my mind...
once I have been somewhere –
even a place that I may not
visit again for days, weeks, months,
even years afterwards –
I have always been able to
accurately navigate myself
back to where I was
with more clarity of memory
than if I were to attempt
to recall a dream...
once I have been somewhere,
I always create a connection to somewhere
that I can use, whenever I need,
to guide me back, as if I could
literally, and effortlessly, step back in time.

I have always been a dreamer...
I have always been hopeful
that the future will be something
that is always worth living for...
I have always loved my family,
and I have always loved
being inspired by people,
and by extraordinary experiences
that I have shared with significant others...

I have always looked forwards,
and I have always looked backwards –
because the future and the past
are always communicating
with one another,
and it has always been at the intersection
between these two extremes
where I have always found
the words to describe
what I feel with every fiber of my being
at a given moment
of pure poetic power...
I have always wanted to give back
more than I have received –
and throughout my life's journey
I have given a part of myself
to those whom I have met,
whom I have known,
whom I have inspired,
who have inspired me in return,
whether they know it or not –
because, all my life, I have been,
and I always shall be,
someone who is meant to
shine a light for those to follow –
like a lighthouse keeper,
a messenger, a traveler,
a navigator,
or, as I like to think of myself as,
a pathfinder.

# Contents

# MARK HASTINGS

Mark Hastings is a poet, writer, podcaster,
from the United Kingdom, who is the author
of fifteen books of poetry, short-stories, novellas,
and who loves nothing more than being inspired.
All his life Mark has been a dreamer and a hopeful
optimist who has always tried to see the best in people
and who has always strived to inspire others
to believe in themselves.

Get Mark's poetry collections:

**_Poet of the Sphere_**

**_Poet of the Sphere – Rising Star (ebook)_**

**_The Sound of Mark_**

**_The Eternal Boy_**

**_The Dreamer and The Dreamer_**

**_Truly Madly Deeply_**

**_The Rambler_**

**_Poet of the Multiverse_**

**_The Comeback Kid_**

Get Mark's short-story
and anthology collections:

**_Too Close To The Sun_**

**_Playing God_**

Get Mark's novella

**_The Doorman_**

Get the books from Mark's

*The Wolf and the Vampire King* book series:

**The Wolf in Me**

**The Wolf in You**

**Vega – The Vampire King**

**The Wolf in Us**

as eBooks or in Paperback at:

Amazon.com

Amazon.co.uk

Printed in Great Britain
by Amazon